Discovering Cities

Liverpool

Liver and Port of Liverpool Buildings
and George's Dock Ventilation Tower
© Mersey Partnership

Albert Dock
© Mersey Partnership

Liverpool's public art: Superlambanana
© Mersey Partnership

Metropolitan Cathedral
© Mersey Partnership

Anglican Cathedral
© Mersey Partnership

Ferry 'Cross the Mersey
© Mersey Partnership

Chinese Arch, Chinatown
© Mersey Partnership

Liverpool John Lennon Airport
© Mersey Partnership

Discovering Cities

Liverpool

Janet Speake and Vivien Fox
Liverpool Hope University

Series Editors
Peter S. Fox and
Christopher M. Law

Geographical
Association

Preface

© Mersey Partnership

The variety and complexity of cities as revealed in their built form has been a source of fascination to the local resident and visitor alike. Can a clear spatial structure be discerned? Why do activities cluster in distinctive quarters or zones? How do relict features throw light on the constantly evolving city? For a long time, human geographers, regional economists, urban sociologists and local historians have sought to understand the processes which shape the city. The growth (or decline) of the city is affected by local, regional and global economic forces. The forces which shape the internal structure of the city are many and varied. There is a market in land that influences the pattern of land use and change. Public policies are often significant but can be complex to understand and difficult to follow. Social factors such as those of class and ethnic community identities are also important.

Written by urban geographers with vast knowledge and experience of the city in question, *Discovering Cities* gathers these issues together in concise and practical guides, illustrated with colour maps and photographs, to enable an enhanced perspective of cities of the British Isles.

Peter S. Fox, Chilwell School, Chilwell, Nottingham

Christopher M. Law, Visiting Fellow, University of Salford, and Research Associate, University of Gloucestershire

Acknowledgements

The authors would like to thank Dr Duncan Light, Liverpool Hope University, for his contribution to the development of the town trails.

© Janet Speake and Vivien Fox, 2006

ISBN 1 84377 133 0
First published 2006
Impression number 10 9 8 7 6 5 4 3 2 1
Year 2008 2007 2006

Published by the Geographical Association,
160 Solly Street, Sheffield S1 4BF.
Website: www.geography.org.uk
E-mail: ga@geography.org.uk

The Geographical Association is a registered charity: no 313129.

The Publications Officer of the GA would be happy to hear from other potential authors who have ideas for geography books. You may contact the Officer via the GA at the address above. The views expressed in this publication are those of the author and do not necessarily represent those of the Geographical Association.

Editing: Rose Pipes
Design and typesetting: Gloss Solutions, Dewsbury
Cartography: Paul Coles
Printing and binding: In China, through Colorcraft Ltd, Hong Kong

Contents

© Mersey Partnership

Introduction

Figure 1: The site and situation of Liverpool.

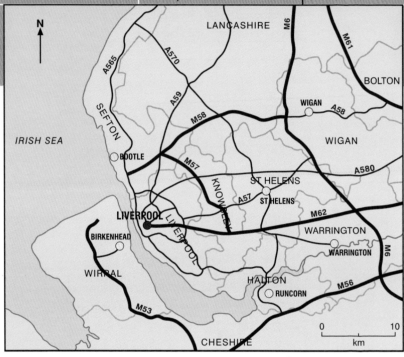

© Janet Speake/Vivien Fox

Liverpool, a city of over 400,000 people within the conurbation of Merseyside (population 1.4 million), is currently experiencing one of its many periods of transition and transformation. It has entered the twenty-first century with renewed confidence, vision and a determination to enhance its status as one of the world's great cities.

In the popular imagination, Liverpool is generally associated with music, sport and, more recently, its creative industries and redeveloped waterfront – now designated as a World Heritage Site. It is also recognised as a once-major world port where de-industrialisation and restructuring at the end of the last century were linked to serious economic decline and associated social problems. Today, signs of the city's regeneration and 're-visioning' are evident everywhere

in the built environment, and in the increasing amount of inward investment in a range of economic sectors. A clear sign of the city's renaissance is its having been awarded the title of European Capital of Culture 2008.

The Merseyside conurbation, of which the city of Liverpool is the core (Figure 1), is largely the product of the Industrial Revolution, and one of the UK's four great provincial industrial metropolises – the others being the West Midlands, Greater Manchester and Strathclyde. Flowing through the heart of the conurbation is the River Mersey, whose navigable estuary sited on the west coast of Britain made it the natural gangway to the Irish Sea and, beyond that, the Atlantic Ocean. This natural advantage was crucial to Liverpool's development as a maritime city and Trans-Atlantic trade port.

Historical geography

Contents

nnine Waterways

teve Howe/B&W Picture Place

The Mersey Estuary.

Urban origins

Much of Liverpool's early history is obscure. While there is evidence of a Bronze Age settlement at Calderstones, it did not feature as a Roman settlement nor was Liverpool named in the Domesday Survey of 1087, although it was probably one of the berewicks (sub manors) attached to the manor of West Derby. The earliest known reference to Liverpool by name occurs in 1192. The derivation of its name has been widely debated, although the 'pool' element almost certainly links to the sheltered tidal creek on the north shore of the River Mersey by which the medieval settlement of Liverpool was sited. In 1207 the borough of Liverpool was created by royal charter, after which its population rose and its port functions began to evolve. Even in the early 1600s Liverpool was comparatively small, with a population of no more than 2000.

Port development

The River Mersey has a funnel- or bottle-shaped estuarine profile and provides a navigable channel for sea-going ships.

The narrow 'neck' of the estuary results in a tidal scour that keeps the channel open, making it possible for shipping lanes to remain operative for hundreds of years with only minimal need for dredging.

In its growth as a port, Liverpool's development was concentrated on the 'pool'. A plateau of higher and firm ground, formed by a series of Triassic sandstone ridges running north to south both to the east and west of the River Mersey, provided suitable development land adjacent to the 'pool' for the industrial and residential premises associated with the growth of the port. Some of the building materials for these early developments, and later for the Anglican Cathedral, came from local sandstone quarries, such as Woolton Quarry.

Access to, and later trade for, the port was hampered by poorly drained land and marshes east of the sandstone ridges in what is now Knowsley. During the medieval period, Chester on the River Dee, with more favourable accessibility, developed as the main port

© Mersey Partnership

Liverpool 1775.

Engraved for The Modern Universal British Traveller

View of LIVERPOOL in Lancashire.

for the region rather than Liverpool. However, by the end of the seventeenth century the Dee was progressively silting up while the marshes surrounding Liverpool were drained. Consequently the predominantly Irish Sea trade (with Wales, the Isle of Man and Ireland) gradually transferred from Chester to Liverpool.

Rapid expansion of trade between Liverpool, North America and the West Indies started in the mid seventeenth century and made Liverpool the pre-eminent port in the region. However, this expansion placed immense pressure on the existing port facilities and extensive regulations had to be introduced to ensure safe and efficient running of the port. By the early eighteenth century it was necessary for Liverpool to improve its facilities for shipping and a series of Acts of Parliament granted permission for the construction of new docks. The first of these, the 'Old Dock', opened in 1715 with space for between 80 and 100 ships. It was an immediate success and gave Liverpool a competitive edge over its rivals Bristol and London. The port of Liverpool (Figure 2) served a hinterland

that extended from mid Wales to Yorkshire and from Staffordshire to Cumbria.

An additional impetus to trade was the opening of the Leeds and Liverpool Canal in 1816 which provided the port with even greater access to its Lancashire and Yorkshire markets and suppliers. With the addition of this canal to the extensive network of inland waterways covering the industrial areas of the wider region, Liverpool became a major nodal point in the canal system. For example, through access to the Trent and Mersey Canal Liverpool was linked to the Potteries and East Midlands, while the Weaver Navigation provided access to the salt extraction and chemical industries of mid Cheshire.

Successive dock construction south and north of the 'Old Dock' extended the waterfront. By 1857, when the Mersey Docks and Harbour Board was established, a total of 21 docks had been built and the area of docks extended approximately 10km from south to north. By the 1870s further expansion of trade had rendered existing

Stanley Dock.

© Pennine Waterways

provision inadequate and additional docks such as the Canada Dock and Harrington Dock were constructed.

Allied with the expansion of the port was the development of associated industries such as shipbuilding and the processing of imported goods such as tobacco, sugar and timber. Warehouses in which imported materials were stored became a distinctive feature of the Liverpool waterfront skyline (e.g. the Tobacco Warehouse at Stanley Dock). Many grand commercial buildings were constructed to house further service industries associated with the port, such as the headquarters of shipping lines, shipping brokers, specialist insurance companies, import and export industries and the Cotton Exchange. To improve communications, an overhead railway was opened in 1893 which ran parallel to the docks from Dingle in the south to Seaforth in the north.

A challenge to the dominance of the port of Liverpool came from Manchester with the opening of the Manchester Ship Canal in 1894. This terminated at docks in the south-west of Manchester and gave direct access to the Mersey at Eastham. Manchester merchants could

therefore by-pass Liverpool and its comparatively expensive dock charges. Thus the port of Liverpool was forced to cut dock charges and as a consequence retained its trade, while Manchester only slowly gained business and did not make profits for many years.

Colonialism and the 'triangular trade'

In the mid seventeenth century Liverpool developed trading links with the West Indies and North America which were associated with colonial expansion. By 1750 it had become the leading participant (exceeding the involvement of Bristol and London) in the notorious, but at the time financially lucrative, 'triangular trade', whereby manufactured goods were shipped from Liverpool to West Africa where they were traded for slaves who were then taken to the West Indies and North America. There they were sold and the profits either returned directly to Liverpool or invested, for example in sugar, rum and cotton which were shipped back to Liverpool. Between 1709 and 1737 it is estimated that the number of Liverpool ships increased from 84 to 171 and that many of these were engaged in the triangular trade. Until the cessation of the slave trade in 1807 the triangular trade contributed substantially

Rodney Street Georgian housing.

to Liverpool's developing wealth. After this date, since slavery itself was not abolished until 1833, the trade between Liverpool and the West Indies continued but with the emphasis on goods (e.g. palm oil) rather than people.

A northern triangular run offered an alternative opportunity for merchants who did not wish to participate in the slave trade. Salt was transported from Liverpool to Newfoundland where it was traded for cod which was then shipped to the West Indies where it was exchanged for coffee and sugar which were then returned to Liverpool.

The American War of Independence (1775-1782) proved disastrous for Liverpool's economy but its prosperity returned in the aftermath, with a surge in demand for American products and trade associated with the Industrial Revolution in the UK.

Liverpool: A pre-eminent Georgian and Victorian city

At the end of the seventeenth century Liverpool had a population of about 6000. When visiting in 1698, Celia Feinnes described it as 'London in miniature,' with 'new built houses of brick and stone after the London fashion' (Morris, 1984). By 1800 Liverpool had become a town of 80,000 people. Large areas of terraced housing had been constructed in the vicinity of the docks and newly industrialising areas to meet the demand for inexpensive housing for workers. From its early core by 'the pool' Liverpool started to spread southwards and the affluent residents sought elegant Georgian houses in areas such as Mount Pleasant. Much of Liverpool's finest architecture dates from this time.

During the nineteenth century Liverpool's population surged, reaching 376,000 in 1851. The reasons for this were, first, in-migration from depopulating, economically-depressed rural regions of England, Wales and Ireland because of the substantial employment opportunities offered by the town, and second, the arrival of emigrants from across Europe en route to North America and elsewhere who decided to stay in the town. The rich cultural heritage of the city is largely linked to this period and is well documented in the city's Maritime Museum.

Walker Art Gallery.

© Mersey Partnership

With a well-connected infrastructure provided by river, canals, radial roads and railways, Liverpool became the transport hub of Merseyside. Routes connected the port to its hinterland and the town spread outwards to subsume many of the surrounding settlements such as Everton and Toxteth. The development of the railway network dates from 1830 when the first passenger railway line opened between Liverpool and Manchester. The opening of the Liverpool and Southport Railway in 1848 encouraged the development of residential suburbs such as Crosby and Formby to the north of the town. Later, in 1886, the Mersey Railway and rail tunnel under the Mersey opened and encouraged residential development 'across the water' in places like Hoylake and West Kirby on the Wirral. The establishment of the overall railway network created opportunities for exclusive suburban development in areas such as Grassendale and Mossley Hill, and by 1895 suburbanisation had extended the city boundary to incorporate former village settlements such as Walton, Woolton, West Derby and Gateacre.

During the Victorian era Liverpool developed swiftly as a financial and insurance centre with companies such as Royal Insurance being established to support its port and industrial enterprises. A clearly identifiable financial quarter evolved in the area around Water Street and many impressive Victorian office buildings were constructed to reflect the town's affluence and prestige. In the city centre retailing became prominent and Liverpool's Victorian civic and cultural confidence was also reflected in the construction of imposing buildings such as the Public Library (the first in England), the Walker Art Gallery, St George's Hall and the University of Liverpool. In common with other large and rapidly-expanding cities, Liverpool encountered social and environmental challenges. Measures to mitigate these included the designation of the world's first Public Health Officer (Dr Duncan), attempts to improve public health, e.g. through piping water from Lake Vyrnwy in Wales, and the creation of public parks, e.g. Sefton Park, Newsham Park and Stanley Park. In 1880 Liverpool received city status by royal charter.

© Mersey Partnership

The liner era waterfront.

© National Archives

The liner era

One of the key features of Liverpool's development during the latter part of the nineteenth and early twentieth centuries was the emergence of the city as a centre for sea-going passenger trade, as well as freight. From the 1840s new shipping lines such as Cunard, White Star and Inman expanded. These lines pioneered the development of large, fast ships for long (often Trans-Atlantic) routes. Between them they carried thousands of emigrants from Europe to North America and other destinations. For the more affluent traveller they became synonymous with luxury travel. At the peak of the liner era, from 1910 to the 1930s, purpose-built hotels (for example the Adelphi) and other facilities such as Riverside Station (Pier Head) served this distinctive market.

Some of the world's most famous liners – the *Queen Mary, Lusitania, Mauritania* (Cunard Line), *Titanic* and *Majestic* (White Star Line) – were Liverpool ships. Many held the Blue Ribband for the fastest crossing of the Atlantic, although from the early twentieth century onwards most luxury liners have sailed from Southampton rather than Liverpool (in order to capture more of the European market).

Port and industrial decline

Until the end of the First World War Liverpool maintained its position as one of the UK's leading ports. However, after the war the city's dependence on its maritime activities and traditional industrial base began to diminish. Contributors to this decline included a general reduction in the UK's global trade, with a shift in focus away from the North Atlantic to Europe; de-industrialisation; the decline of traditional manufacturing industries; and changing technologies in port activities (e.g. containerisation).

Liverpool was severely affected by these changes; the volume of shipping and trade passing through the port fell, the number of dock workers dropped, general levels of unemployment rose, and traditional port-associated industries declined, as did the city's economy.

Figure 3: The electoral districts of Liverpool.
Source: Boundary Committee for England, 2003.

Mid to late twentieth century transitions

From the 1930s onwards many initiatives were introduced to tackle Liverpool's economic and social problems. The government intervened by giving privileged status to the area so that investors would have financial incentives to set up businesses, thereby addressing the problem of high unemployment levels in the city. The city's physical infrastructure (especially the dock area) was badly affected during the bombing raids of the Second World War, and the de-centralisation of economic activity and population, aided by an improved transport infrastructure including the Queensway road tunnel under the River Mersey, was a major feature of this government intervention.

Poverty in the inner city slums.

In the 1930s and 1940s large industrial and housing estates were created within the city boundary at Speke and Aintree and outside the city boundary to the north east at Kirkby. These estates successfully attracted international manufacturing companies to the city such as Dunlop (rubber goods), ICI (chemicals and metals), Lockheed (aircraft components) and Ford (motor vehicles).

In 1966 the City Council approved a programme of slum clearance within the city centre with a remit to clear 78,000 residential properties. Planned large-scale redevelopment of the inner city was accompanied by the construction of several sizable estates in peripheral areas including Kirkby, Croxteth and Netherley. These suburban estates contained largely high-density (frequently high-rise) municipal housing.

However, by maintaining a largely industrially-orientated economic base the city was vulnerable to recession which, when it hit in the late 1960s, resulted in mass redundancies and consequent hardship for many of the inhabitants. The city's population declined at this time, and unlike some other cities where people migrated from the industrial areas to the suburbs and surrounding smaller towns, in the case of Liverpool people tended to leave the Merseyside area completely. The high level of net outward migration had an adverse effect on the city's demography, one characteristic of which was a falling birth rate.

The city's severe economic problems were exacerbated by rising levels of poverty and social disadvantage. The bold attempts of the mid twentieth century to improve the built fabric of the city were thrown into question as environmental, social and economic problems in the peripheral estates triggered the need for extensive renewal and refurbishment. Inner city decline continued in a downward spiral and was compounded by the fact that the City Council was experiencing major financial difficulties. In 1982, at the depths of the recession and at the height of political and social unrest, riots occurred in the inner city area of Toxteth. The city and its problems were catapulted into the national and international gaze and the search for solutions became imperative.

Becoming a twenty-first century city

Contents

Table 1: Unemployment in Liverpool, 1971-2001.
Sources: Liverpool City Council (1993; 2005)
and www.statistics.gov.uk.

Year	Number	%	UK%
1971	28,666	10.6	3.8
1981	46,812	20.4	5.6
1991	41,129	21.6	9.0
2001	19,421	6.0	3.4

The post-industrial legacy

'Liverpool from seaport to e-port' describes succinctly the nature of the city's transition in just 100 years, from a port founded on the trade in material goods, to a port based on the electronic transfer of knowledge and information. Such a transition has not, however, been achieved without considerable painful adjustment. In Liverpool, as in other former industrially-orientated port cities, transformation in the mid to late twentieth century has been largely a consequence of de-industrialisation, globalisation and shifts in the international division of labour. For Liverpool the impacts of economic decline were particularly severe, mainly because of its dependency on traditional employment sectors and lack of economic diversification. Its location in an economically-weakened region exacerbated its downward spiral. The inner city, once the industrial engine, bore the full force of the industrial collapse. The impacts of economic recession manifested themselves in the radically altered physical environment typified by large areas of vacant and derelict land, and changed demographic and socio-economic structures. As a result, distinctive and challenging geographies of disadvantage emerged within the city.

Geographies of disadvantage

As Liverpool's traditional secondary-sector industries collapsed and rates of job loss rose, a comparatively underdeveloped and slowly growing tertiary sector could not compensate for high levels of employment contraction. Consequently, unemployment levels in the city soared.

Between 1971 and 1981 the unemployment rate in Liverpool doubled to 20.4% (see Table 1) and although it decreased in the next decade the rate was still twice the UK average. Unemployment levels were particularly high in inner city wards (e.g. 37.6% in Everton in 1981) and marginally lower in outer city council estates (e.g. 32% in Speke in 1981). Even by 1991 nearly half of the workforce in the former ward of Everton and Vauxhall were unemployed, although by 2001 unemployment levels had fallen substantially to 9% and 6% respectively. Nevertheless, while still broadly comparable to an overall rate of 6% in the city, unemployment figures across the city were higher than the UK average of 3.4%. Increasing levels of social polarisation became evident as the gap in unemployment levels widened between the poorest areas of the inner city and the more affluent wards in the south of the city such as Grassendale, Childwall and Woolton.

Table 2: Population change, 1971-2001.
Sources: Fox (1996), Liverpool City Council (1993),
www.statistics.gov.uk.

	Liverpool			Merseyside		
Year	Population	Net loss	% change	Population	Net loss	% change
1971	610,114	n/a	n/a	1,656,500	n/a	n/a
1981	516,700	93,414	−15.3	1,503,120	153,380	−9.3
1991	474,522	42,178	−8.2	1,366,884	136,236	−9.3
2001	439,473	35,049	−7.9	1,362,034	4,850	−0.4

Because of the city's historic reliance on industrial employment, Liverpool had a higher level of semi-skilled and unskilled workers than the UK average, a characteristic which prevailed throughout the last quarter of the twentieth century. For example, in 1981 36% of workers were classified as semi-skilled and unskilled, compared with 27% in the UK as a whole. The city's comparative position has not measurably improved since, and the greatest concentrations of these socio-economic groups are still to be found in inner city wards. Measures taken to address this position include placing emphasis on raising educational aspirations within the city and re-skilling the workforce.

Population restructuring

The contraction of employment opportunities in Liverpool throughout the latter decades of the twentieth century contributed to a decrease in population in the city that was one of the most severe in the UK. Between 1971 and 2001 Liverpool's population fell by 27.9% from 610,114 to 439,473. The most substantial decrease (-93,414) took place between 1971 and 1981 when economic recession was most intense. Contrary to general belief, the recession and depopulation were not confined to Liverpool, but were conurbation-wide (see Table 2). Some districts within the conurbation, e.g. Knowsley, had even higher population losses than Liverpool. Although some people may have moved within the

conurbation in search of employment, the overall outcome was a substantial net loss of population and a declining birth rate. By 2001, the decline had started to diminish in Liverpool and had almost halted across Merseyside as a whole.

The inner city was hit hardest. Between 1971 and 1981 two inner city wards formerly named Granby and Melrose each lost 36% of their population and several others, such as the former Abercromby and Vauxhall wards, declined by almost a third. Several outer city housing estates, such as Speke and Netherley, experienced losses on a similar scale. In the immediate aftermath of this most severe phase of recession there was a general slowing of population decline. However, there were some notable exceptions. The inner city ward of Everton experienced a population loss of 7703 (-54.4%).

Between 1991 and 2001 this population loss tapered and by 2003 the city recorded its first, albeit small, population increase in 70 years.

Associated with substantial economic decline has been a demographic restructuring. In part, this is due to economically-active age groups seeking employment opportunities elsewhere. This was mirrored in the population profile for 2001 when 38.5% of Liverpool's population were within the 30-59 age category compared with

Obsolete former industrial buildings remain today.

41.5% nationally. The contrast is even more stark for inner city wards, such as the former Granby ward, where just 34.4% came in this category.

Environmental degradation

Accompanying the direct socio-economic consequences of recession were rapid changes in the built environment. Derelict, vacant and functionally obsolete former industrial buildings and land characterised much of the inner city. The extent of this degraded land, its fragmentation and the cost of restoration were such that potential investors were deterred.

Interspersed with the former industrial land and surviving businesses were substantial tracts of old, obsolete, often sub-standard, traditional terraced housing. This, combined with largely unsuccessful attempts to redevelop inner-city housing in the mid twentieth century (e.g. through the construction of high rise blocks in areas such as Everton and Netherley), created a depressed property market and posed serious development challenges.

Quality of life

The *Quality of Life Report* published by the City Council in 1991 found that 40% of Liverpool's population lived in poverty and 15% lived in intense poverty. This survey defined poverty as:

'...being unable to afford a way of life which most people in society would consider to be the minimum acceptable. To be unable to afford three or more socially-determined necessities is to live in poverty. To be unable to afford seven or more means cutting back in all areas of life and experiencing a life of intense poverty' (Liverpool City Council, 1991).

These levels were twice those of equivalent national levels reported in the 1990 Breadline Britain Survey (Frayman, 1991). Vulnerable groups included the unemployed (72% in poverty), lone-adult families (68% in poverty) and Council tenants (68% in poverty). Although poverty was widespread across the city there was also clear polarisation in the degree of poverty. In the most deprived areas (four inner city wards and two

Garden Festival site.

© Liverpool Daily Post & Echo Syndication Dept

outer estate wards) 63% of households were in poverty compared with 17% in the least deprived suburban wards. Other key characteristics of poverty in the poorest areas included the lowest incomes in the city (just 41% of the city average) and high levels of income support (40%). In lone-adult families 80% lived in poverty and 57% in intense poverty. In all, almost a quarter of households considered that their health had not been good over the previous year and that their general situation had declined over the previous five years.

During the 1990s poverty continued to be a major problem facing Liverpool. The multi-faceted nature of poverty warranted concerted efforts on the part of agencies such as local and central government, voluntary and private sectors, with the implementation of an effective anti-poverty strategy being an objective of paramount importance.

Measures to counter disadvantage

The consequence of the recession and its impacts was the emergence of a markedly different Liverpool. While it was clear that the industrial era was essentially over, the character of a post-industrial Liverpool was almost totally unimagined in the 1960s. It was evident that there were major issues to be addressed surrounding the nature of future economic revival and the type of jobs which could be created in order to stem the population loss. Two key questions predominated: what sort of a city *would* Liverpool be? And what kind of city *could* it be?

Regeneration initiatives

As a result of the Inner Areas study of the early 1970s, from 1972 onwards a range of inner area and urban programmes were introduced nationally to tackle urban renewal through such measures as derelict land grants and city grants. During the 1970s and 1980s, Liverpool, like many former industrial/port cities, was at the forefront in its attempts to regenerate run-down urban core areas and experienced the impacts of these national funding schemes. The city also received spatially targeted assistance to revitalise specially identified areas (Figure 4), leading to the establishment of the Merseyside Development Corporation (1981-97) to tackle waterfront improvements, the Enterprise Zone at Speke-Garston, and the Freeport at Seaforth which sought to

Figure 4: Early regeneration areas.

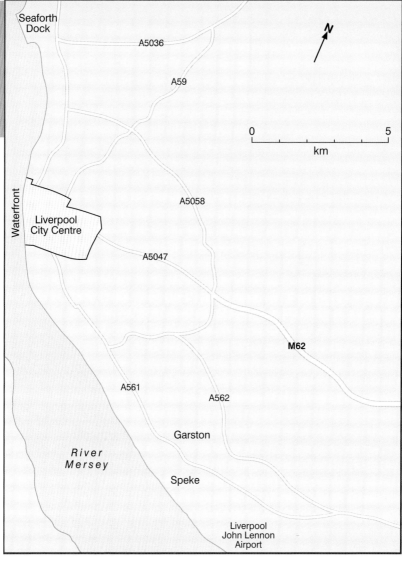

stimulate economic activity. Many other initiatives of the 1980s, such as the 1984 Liverpool International Garden Festival, focused on the re-use and treatment of vacant, contaminated and derelict land, and environmental improvement.

The targeting of assistance continued in the early 1990s when Liverpool participated in the bidding rounds of City Challenge. In the first round, in 1990, Liverpool City Council was one of 11 local authorities whose bids were successful. A key element of City Challenge was the use of public funds to encourage further investment by the private sector. The Single Regeneration Budget (SRB), introduced in 1994, became the main source of central

Urban Splash Tea Factory.

© Janet Speake/Vivien Fox

government support for regeneration and brought with it a wider-ranging, more co-ordinated approach to Liverpool's renewal.

The city also became fully engaged with bidding for European Union funds. In 1994, as part of the wider area of Merseyside, Liverpool became eligible for EU Objective 1 funding on the basis that its GDP per head was less than 75% of the EU average. As a consequence, the Merseyside region received £630 million between 1994 and 1999. Key projects included Rope Walks, Princes Dock and improvements to Liverpool John Lennon Airport.

Recently, the region was designated as an Objective 1 area for 2000-2006 and it is anticipated that Merseyside will benefit from a £2 billion investment programme that will include £844 million from the EU. This investment will be directed towards the development of business, people, locations, and Pathway communities. Under Objective 1, eight Strategic Investment Areas have been designated, including Speke-Halewood, Eastern Approaches, Atlantic Gateway and the City Centre.

Throughout recent decades, the improvement of housing in the city has also been the focus of many, often innovative, initiatives such as the Eldonians in Vauxhall, and by Barratts in the vicinity of Liverpool University. Urban Splash, a development company established in the early 1990s, has contributed substantially to the revitalisation of the housing sector within the city centre through projects such as the Tea Factory.

Revitalising Liverpool

In addition to tackling problems arising out of the recession, Liverpool has had to address the challenge of reinventing itself in the context of an agenda set by a new world economic order defined by globalisation, the information and communication revolution, and the rise of the knowledge economy. The challenge was for the city to identify its strengths and weaknesses and create a vision for its future.

In many ways Liverpool's programme of revitalisation has been similar to that adopted in most Western economies. For example, in the 1970s and 1980s the

Albert Dock.

emphasis was on environmental improvement in conjunction with a recognition of the importance of heritage. By the 1990s and early 2000s the emphasis was on culture, community and knowledge. The following section explores the nature and impacts of the process of revitalisation on the city's waterfront.

Rediscovering the waterfront

By the late 1970s the condition of Liverpool's waterfront had seriously deteriorated. Characterised by functional obsolescence, many of the docks were disused and neglected. The approximately 10km stretch of defunct dockyards and manufacturing industries faced the city with an immense challenge, and infilling and demolition (including the Albert Dock) were among the suggested options.

The scale of the challenge was reflected in the measures taken to address the problem by the Conservative government of the time. Through selective targeting of funds such as Derelict Land Grants, and through the activity of the Merseyside Development Corporation and various partnerships, substantial land restoration was achieved.

Inspired by waterfront regeneration in Baltimore and Boston, USA, the revitalisation of the historic Albert Dock provided commercial and residential premises, was a flagship for Liverpool's waterfront regeneration, and became a popular visitor attraction (with over 6 million visitors by the end of the 1980s) as part of the city's attempt to promote tourism in the city.

Site improvements and the creation of investment opportunities elsewhere in the waterfront area led to extensive functional and aesthetic change. Transformations included the creation of the Brunswick Dock Business Park, the Liverpool Marina and the Water Sport Centre. In addition, there have been significant building conversions and new-build for residential purposes (e.g. Coburg Quay).

In recent years transformation of the northern docks (to the north of Pier Head) has continued apace, including the development of new hotels (at Princes Dock) and the conversion of the Waterloo Dock warehouse into apartments.

Liverpool FC's ground at Anfield.

© Liverpool Football Club

Other regeneration initiatives were also undertaken alongside the river. During the late 1970s and early 1980s, former industrial and commercial land concentrated around both the present and the disused airport at Speke was regenerated through a combination of an Enterprise Zone and out-of-town retail parks. However, in the late 1980s businesses on these retail parks suffered as a result of the depression in the housing market and decreased demand for home improvements. As a consequence, there were high levels of vacant land and property, which continued to exist for several years. In the late 1990s major new measures were introduced in an attempt to re-regenerate the area. Revitalisation of this part of the city has been driven largely by the Speke-Garston Partnership (started in 1995). Major ventures within this location include the Estuary Business Park and Mersey Retail Park.

The effect of regenerative activity on Liverpool's waterfront has been to transform much of the riverside. In parts the cityscape has shifted from industrial to post-industrial, although there are clear contrasts between the waterfront north and south of Pier Head, and between the narrow belt of regeneration activity next to the river and areas further inland. One of the criticisms often levelled at waterfront initiatives is that they focus regeneration activity on a small locality and contribute little to wider community and physical regeneration. Other apparently 'neglected' areas have been identified in Liverpool's inner city.

The general revival of the central former dockland areas, together with the renaissance of the central area, is steadily making Liverpool an attractive destination for cruise ships and proposals have been made to increase the depth of the water channel to Princes Dock and Pier Head to enable larger ships to dock.

Liverpool was one of the first cities in the UK to implement waterfront regeneration and it is ongoing. As with many regeneration schemes, those in Liverpool's waterfront area exhibit a progressive shift from environmental and heritage-led activities to culturally-led regeneration.

Tate Liverpool.

Culturally-led regeneration

The recognition of the significant role that cultural activities could play in the revitalisation of cities was a distinct feature of the 1990s and early 2000s. For industrial cities such as Liverpool, culturally-led regeneration provided the opportunity to re-image the city and to re-position it in relation to direct competitors. At the end of the twentieth century Liverpool's varied and rich cultural assets were being actively celebrated and promoted within and beyond the city, and in many ways this has contributed to its 're-imaging'.

Liverpool is recognised worldwide for its football tradition and its popular music, especially that of the Beatles. The commodification of the city's culture became increasingly apparent in the 1990s with tourists and residents alike being encouraged to participate in 'hallmark' events such as the Mathew Street Festival, the River Festival and the Tall Ships Race. Each summer the King's Dock has been playing host to the Summer Proms, featuring concerts to suit a wide range of musical tastes (often Liverpool's own bands and orchestras). Such widely promoted events have supplemented the established roles of the city's arts venues such as Tate Liverpool and the Walker Art Gallery. The Magical Mystery Tour to locations associated with the Beatles, such as Penny Lane and Strawberry Fields, is one of a number of attractions which focus on the city's unique cultural heritage.

Concurrently, Liverpool's cityscape has undergone substantial change. The rise of the café-bar culture and the redevelopment of formerly rundown areas, such as Rope Walks with its clubs, bars, restaurants and loft-living, has radically altered the appearance and function of much of the city centre. Many individuals and organisations have become active in the revitalisation of the city centre, including innovative developers such as Urban Splash, Maritime Housing, and numerous public-private partnerships. In many locations, including Wood Street and Concert Square with their varied residential and leisure functions, extended opening hours are making Liverpool increasingly a 24-hour city.

A common feature of recent city regeneration projects is the emphasis on innovative architecture and design, exemplified in Liverpool by the FACT centre (for film, art and creative technology) and the Paradise Project

Everton Football Club, Goodison Park.

© Everton Football Club

based on the former Chavasse Park. It is recognised, however, that such modern developments should not be at the expense of the city's architectural heritage, itself a valuable 'commodity'. Liverpool has many superb examples of Georgian and Victorian architecture, and part of the city – around Pier Head – was awarded World Heritage Site status in 2004.

One consequence of the culture-led and property-led regeneration of the city centre has been a rise in population from around 5000 in 1995 to more than 10,000 in 2004. In part this has been due to gentrification and the progressive 'bourgeoisisation' of enclaves within the city such as Concert Square, and also due to the rapid increase in the number of students at the city's three universities. Several prominent historic buildings in the city centre have been refurbished for student accommodation and the construction of purpose-built student residences has further revitalised the city centre.

Although the most prominent, large-scale, capital-intensive elements of Liverpool's culturally-led regeneration have been within the city centre, cultural revitalisation has been encouraged throughout the city. Local and community focused arts activities have flourished, for example drama productions featuring local residents in celebration of the history of their area or of key features within it (such as the Matchworks – the former Bryant and May match factory – in Garston). Other activities include the involvement of schools in the promotion of art.

Liverpool's identity is closely bound to sport, particularly The Grand National, Open Golf, and football. Liverpool FC and Everton FC are recognised globally as successful clubs synonymous with the city of Liverpool and both contribute to its cultural identity. Discussions associated with potential relocation for both clubs and the construction of state-of-the-art stadia have given prominence to the clubs and the role of sport in the life and future prosperity of the city.

In June 2003 it was announced that Liverpool's bid to be European Capital of Culture in 2008 had been successful. For the city this represented a major step forward in terms of identifying Liverpool in the national and international arena as a creative and dynamic city of, and for, the twenty-first century. The city's designation as City of Culture 2008 has

Continuing development.

already raised awareness of its major strengths as a creative and multi-faceted contemporary city. The Capital of Culture Company has been set up to bring forward investment proposals and organise events, and suggestions have already been made for major and innovative developments.

Celebrating diversity

In common with many large ports, Liverpool has a rich cultural diversity that is increasingly recognised as contributing to the city's dynamism and character. Liverpool is distinctive in having the oldest Chinese community in Europe, plus Somali, Caribbean and Norwegian communities.

In recent years the city's diversity has been recognised and celebrated in myriad ways. One of the most tangible has been the regeneration of Chinatown through the collaborative actions of the community and Rope Walks Partnership. The revitalised area now possesses the largest Chinese Arch in Europe and hosts the city's Chinese New Year celebrations.

The knowledge economy

A key element of Liverpool's change in the 1990s was the recognition of the importance of the learning and knowledge-based economy. In 2003 the number of university students studying in the city reached 40,000 and Liverpool has promoted itself as a City of Learning. This represents a re-orientation of the city's economic focus and an opportunity for knowledge-led revitalisation, one example of which is the development of the National Biomanufacturing Centre at the Estuary Park, Speke. There is a long history of biomanufacturing at Speke, which is home to several major pharmaceutical companies, including those specialising in the production of advanced vaccines. The area has become one of Europe's largest concentrations of biomanufacturers. This, combined with research bases at the city's universities, has made Liverpool one of the most important biochemical centres in Europe.

At Wavertree Technology Park, established in 1983, there is a cluster of information and communication technology (ICT) businesses. Some of the most successful companies have been those involved with the development of computer games and gaming technologies, hence the epithet 'e-port' now often applied to the city. Other ICT clusters are to be found in pockets of the newly-revitalised industrial and commercial premises of the southern

Liverpool John Lennon Airport.

docks (for example Brunswick Dock).

Connections

Liverpool's revival has been enhanced by the upgrading of its road, rail, sea and air connections and generally improved transport infrastructure. Perhaps the most striking feature of Liverpool's resurgent interconnectedness has been the extraordinarily rapid rise in air traffic at Liverpool John Lennon Airport which in 2002 became the fastest growing airport in the UK and one of the fastest growing in Europe. In 2002 the number of passengers travelling through the airport totalled 2.8 million. Recent annual average growth in passenger numbers has been as high as 27% a year (compared with 6% at other airports in the North West) and total numbers are expected to rise to between 3.6 and 5.8 million by 2015. Primarily due to the expansion of the low-cost airlines Easyjet and Ryanair, the volume of international traffic increased by 22% between 1991 and 2000. Since 1991, freight activity has also grown, with the volume of traffic almost doubling.

Since the late 1990s the rise in the importance of Irish Sea links has been reflected in expanded ferry services to Dublin, Belfast and the Isle of Man and in an upswing in the volume of Irish Sea freight transport. This, combined with new freight handling procedures associated with the development of containerisation processes, has contributed to an increase in port activity. Dock facilities are largely concentrated at the port of Liverpool's Seaforth terminal and a smaller volume of trade is conducted in the south of the city at Garston Docks. Improvements to mooring facilities at Princes Dock will increase the number of ships able to dock close to the city centre, including more cruise liners.

Prospects

After half a century in which the city experienced a tumult of decline, collective despondency and wishful remembrance of its former pre-eminence as one of the great eighteenth and nineteenth century cities, Liverpool now appears to have a vision for its future and greater confidence in itself as a major city for the twenty-first century. Like many other western industrial cities, Liverpool is attempting to re-image itself, drawing upon both its past and its present strengths, and is undergoing a rapid economic, social and physical transformation.

Small area studies and trails

Contents

Trail 1.

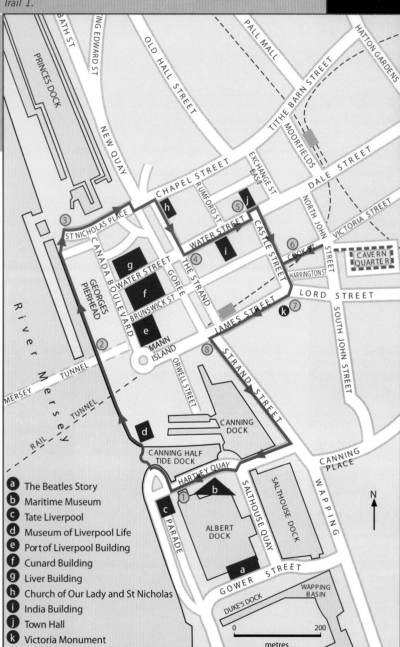

- **a** The Beatles Story
- **b** Maritime Museum
- **c** Tate Liverpool
- **d** Museum of Liverpool Life
- **e** Port of Liverpool Building
- **f** Cunard Building
- **g** Liver Building
- **h** Church of Our Lady and St Nicholas
- **i** India Building
- **j** Town Hall
- **k** Victoria Monument

Introduction

There are many varied and distinctive layers to Liverpool's cityscape, each of which represents a key element of its development. Visiting, observing and interpreting different locations in the city helps to reveal those facets of the city which are unique and those which are found in other large cities that have experienced rapid transformation.

The centre of Liverpool's maritime history.

The following four trails visit contrasting parts of the city and explore them within the context of some key processes and themes. Trails 1, 2 and 3 all take routes through the city centre and look at the city's historical legacy within the context of contemporary urban revitalisation. Trail 1 focuses on Liverpool's maritime heritage, its central waterfront and part of the area now designated as a World Heritage Site. Trail 2 visits the rapidly regenerating area of Rope Walks which is at the core of Liverpool's clubland and residential revival. Trail 3 focuses on the city's impressive architectural inheritance and how current users are (re)interpreting the past for contemporary purposes, e.g. in films and television programmes.

Trails 1 to 3 have been designed so that they can be followed either individually or linked together. Trail 4 links the south and north of the city and compares and contrasts the different ways in which the city has approached its revitalisation. It can also be integrated with Trails 1-3.

Trail 1: Liverpool's maritime heritage

Distance: 2.3km
(3km incl extension)
Walking time: 1 hour 30
(2 hours 30 incl extension)
Disabled access: yes

In 2004 it was announced that the central core of Liverpool's maritime history, centred on the Albert Dock, Pier Head and the financial district, had been awarded the prestigious status of a UNESCO World Heritage Site. The designation gives global recognition to the importance of the city's maritime history and its architectural significance, which will be explored in this trail, together with aspects of the city's recent revitalisation.

1. The tour starts at the Albert Dock. Constructed between 1841 and 1845 (at a cost of £500,000) and designed by the engineer Jesse Hartley, this was the first dock in the world to be completely enclosed.

Tate Liverpool.

© Mersey Partnership

It was closed in 1972 and the buildings and dock became derelict and dilapidated. Between 1984 and 1988 the dock was redeveloped as a tourist attraction, with a variety of functions including numerous shops, apartments, hotels, museums of the city's maritime past and the Beatles, and Tate Liverpool. The latter is of note because Sir Henry Tate (1819-1899) made his wealth through the import and refining of cane sugar in Liverpool and then moved to London where he used his fortune to start the Tate art collections. When the Tate Gallery in London wanted a northern outpost, Liverpool was considered to be the most appropriate venue.

2. Continue northwards along Riverside Walk to the three prominent, large white buildings: the most southerly is the Port of Liverpool Building, the middle one is the Cunard Building and the northern one is the Royal Liver Building. These three buildings are collectively called the 'Three Graces'. The Port of Liverpool Building (1907) was constructed as the headquarters of the Mersey Docks and Harbour Board and is still the administrative base for Mersey

Docks and Harbour Company. The Cunard Building (1916) was constructed for the Cunard shipping line but is now occupied by a number of different companies. The Royal Liver Building (1910) was built for, and remains the headquarters of, the Royal Liver Insurance Company. On top of the building are the famous 'Liver Birds' (a cross between an eagle and a cormorant), one of Liverpool's most famous symbols. It is said that if the Liver Birds ever fly away, Liverpool will no longer exist, so this is why the birds are held down by cables!

Opposite the Liver Building is Pier Head. This was the place from which many of the great liners set sail and in its heyday was a significant transport terminus. It is now used by Mersey Ferries. From here it is possible to take a ferry across the river to view the magnificent waterfront. The direct return trip normally takes about half an hour and the leisure trip about an hour. The landing stage is also used by passenger ships serving the Isle of Man.

Cunard Building.

Just to the north of the Royal Liver Building is a white stone monument, the memorial to the 'Heroes of the Marine Engine Room' – more often known as 'The Titanic Memorial'. It commemorates the loss of engineers in the Titanic disaster of 1912 when c.1500 passengers and crew lost their lives after the liner sank having hit an iceberg off Nova Scotia on her maiden voyage. Looking north is Princes Dock which has been revitalised recently with new developments such as hotels. It is the proposed site for the new pier for ocean-going liners.

3. Turn right into St Nicholas Place, cross The Strand and walk towards The Church of Our Lady and St Nicholas. This church, with its distinctive weather vane in the shape of a sailing ship, is known as the Sailors' Church and dates from 1360, although the body was rebuilt in 1776 and the tower rebuilt in 1815. Turn right along The Strand past the Tower Building (1908). This building stands on the site of a fortified house, the Tower of Liverpool, which used to be the town's gaol (demolished in 1819).

4. Turn left into Water Street. This street is best known for its many fine banking and insurance buildings which were established when the port of Liverpool was at its most prosperous. On the south side of the street notice the India Building (built between 1923 and 1931 by the Blue Funnel Line). If it is open, take a detour through the ground floor which contains a magnificent shopping arcade now serving office workers. On the north side of Water Street are the Oriel Chambers (1864), a building designed by Liverpool architect Peter Ellis and considered as one of the finest cast iron buildings in Europe. The imposing Barclay's Bank (1932) (formerly the head quarters of Martin's Bank) had a very advanced construction and is probably best known for its completely ducted pipes and fine internal wood panelling.

5. Adjacent to Barclay's Bank is the Town Hall which dates from 1754. There have been substantial later additions to the original building, for example the dome and portico. A notable feature is the sculptural representations of animals associated with the parts of the world with which Liverpool had trading links.

Mathew Street.

© Janet Speake/Vivien Fox

© Janet Speake/Vivien Fox

By the Town Hall on Exchange Street West are two red 'listed' telephone kiosks. They were designed by Sir Giles Gilbert Scott, architect of Liverpool Anglican Cathedral, and became familiar throughout the UK during the twentieth century. From the front of the Town Hall turn into Castle Street, former location of many of Liverpool's newspaper offices and the former Bank of England (no.31).

6. *For those interested in Beatles heritage turn left into Cook Street. Walk to the junction of Cook Street with North John Street. Mathew Street and Cavern Walks are visible from this point across North John Street. The Cavern Quarter is centred on the site of the former famous nightclub 'The Cavern' where The Beatles performed in the early 1960s. Close by in Stanley Street is the statue of Eleanor Rigby sculpted by the 1960s' singer Tommy Steele. Return to Castle Street.*

Continue along Castle Street to Derby Square, the site of Liverpool Castle (1235-1721). The large monument in the square is to Queen Victoria.

7. From the Victoria Monument turn right into James Street and walk towards Strand Street past James Street Station (1886). On the right is the red brick and white stone Albion

House (1898). It was designed by Richard Norman Shaw, who also designed the similar-looking Old Scotland Yard near the Houses of Parliament in London. Albion House was originally built as the headquarters of the White Star Line, one of Liverpool's major shipping lines and owner of the fated liner, the RMS Titanic.

8. Cross over The Strand to the street called Mann Island, former location of the Gorée Piazzas warehouses and named after an island off Dakar, Senegal which was reputedly the centre of the Slave Trade. Continue to walk southwards along Strand Street to the entrance to Albert Dock. Enter the dock complex via the pedestrian gateway. This 'setted' pathway passes between Canning Dock and Salthouse Dock (named because of the former Salt Factory located on the north side of Strand Street). At the entrance look back across Strand Street. Just beyond Strand Street was the location of Liverpool's first dock (now filled in and part of the Paradise Street development project). Return to the Albert Dock where the trail began.

Trail 2.

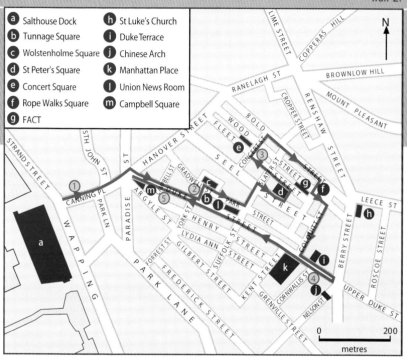

a	Salthouse Dock	**h**	St Luke's Church
b	Tunnage Square	**i**	Duke Terrace
c	Wolstenholme Square	**j**	Chinese Arch
d	St Peter's Square	**k**	Manhattan Place
e	Concert Square	**l**	Union News Room
f	Rope Walks Square	**m**	Campbell Square
g	FACT		

Trail 2: Clubland and prestige living

Distance: 3.6km
Walking time: 2 hours
Disabled access: Yes, but while the roads between Duke Street and Bold Street are narrow and easy to cross, beware of vehicles such as delivery vans. Not all kerbs are at grade and some may be too high for wheelchair users.

One of the most vibrant parts of the city centre is that known as Rope Walks. Since the 1990s this area has been a key focus for much of the city's innovative, culturally-led urban renaissance. It lies between the waterfront and the main retail area and was formerly a centre for traditional maritime industry such as ropemaking for sailing ships and dock activities. The canyon-like streets with enclosing tall buildings provided extensive warehousing, reflecting the spatial requirements of the rope laying (twisting) and stretching processes.

The area is also a very good example of a liminal landscape. Liminal spaces are those in a state of transition or transformation. For example, it might be the space of transition between one social grouping and another, or from one market area to another, or between one physical use and another, or any combination of such transformations.

Through the activities of the Rope Walks Partnership in the 1990s the area came to epitomise regeneration associated with the creative industries, and became the heart of the city's clubland. Associated with the economic transformation of the area has been the construction of new apartments and the conversion of older buildings for residential and restaurant use, with most residents being young and single.

The heart of Liverpool's vibrant clubland.

© Jefferson's Air Photography.

1. From the Albert Dock walk to Strand Street and cross at the pedestrian crossing, continuing to the junction with Canning Place and on to Hanover Street. On the corner of Hanover Street and Duke Street is an imposing red brick former office and warehouse, built in 1890 for the shipowners Ellis and Co. At the main junction turn right into Duke Street and walk eastwards up the hill to Tunnage Square (a new pedestrian route 'punched' across the grain of the Rope Walks streets as part of a series of linked public spaces planned for the area).

2. Go left through Tunnage Square into Wolstenholme Square with its bold and colourful modern public art. Low land values and obsolete warehouse properties attracted car parking and low-investment night-time leisure use to this area, which typified a blighted urban landscape. As land values increased during the early 2000s, master plans for the area started to be put into effect. Buildings have been cleared or refurbished, vacant sites have been developed, and new uses have come into the area.

Turn right into Parr Street and follow it to the junction with Slater Street. Turn left into Slater Street and then right into Seel Street, crossing over the road to enter St Peter's Square. St Peter's Church (1788) is the oldest Roman Catholic Church in Liverpool but has now been refurbished for mixed commercial use. St Peter's Square brings a contrast to the streetscape, offering a route through to the Tea Factory on Fleet Street.

The Tea Factory, constructed c.1930, is a conversion scheme by the development company Urban Splash

© Chris Tubbs

Concert Square.

© Janet Speake/Vivien Fox

and offers space for offices, workshops, creative and performing arts, and apartments. From here, turn left along Fleet Street and follow the incline down to Concert Square.

3. Concert Square is now one of the hubs of Liverpool's clubland. It comprises mixed-use buildings with mostly bars and clubs on lower floors and apartments above. Its development was initiated by Urban Splash and was one of the city's earliest attempts at culturally-led regeneration. Turn right at Concert Square into Concert Street and continue to Bold Street.

Bold Street's character is one of an edge-of-city-centre shopping street with small independent units now housing specialist shops or shops catering for the increasing number of apartment dwellers. Looking to the right, the ruined shell of St Luke's Church (1802), bombed during the Second World War, provides a strong focal point in the area and is a well-established landmark in this part of the city. Walking up Bold Street

towards St Luke's Church you will reach Rope Walks Square.

Turn right into the square and head towards the FACT centre on Wood Street. The FACT (Foundation for Art and Creative Technology) centre (2003) was built at a cost of £10 million. It has three cinemas, art galleries and a café-bar. From the centre turn left into Wood Street and right into Colquitt Street where you will see a large brown brick building on the right. This was the home of the Royal Institution (1799), established to promote science, art and literature. When the Institution moved to London, the Liverpool building closed and is now used as office space, currently for a national children's charity. Also on Colquitt Street are several new residential blocks, e.g. Manoli's Yard, and building conversions.

Continue along Colquitt Street to Duke Street (northern side). Just on your left on Duke Street is a courtyard entered through high gates, containing a tall, narrow block

Union News Room.

of houses called Duke Terrace. Recent renovation work has taken place on this only surviving example of back-to-back housing in Liverpool. During the nineteenth century many people lived in houses like this which were often overcrowded and unhealthy, there being no water supply or sanitation.

Return to Duke Street, turn left and continue uphill to the Chinese Arch at the junction of Duke Street and Nelson Street. Completed in 2000, the arch is a focal point for Liverpool's Chinatown which is reputedly the oldest Chinatown in Europe. The surrounding streets show many examples of 'heritagisation', for example bilingual street signs (English and Chinese) and dragon designs on the street lamps. The large church adjacent to the arch has been converted into an art gallery. One of the features of this urban nucleus is the great variety of businesses operating within it.

4. Return back along Duke Street on the southern side. Just beyond Cornwallis Street on your left you may want to explore the linked courts of Manhattan Place, an interesting blend of College buildings, apartments and restaurants. Return to Duke Street and continue downhill past the imposing former Union News Room building (at 105 Duke Street).

5. As you approach the junction of Duke Street with Hanover Street look out for Campbell Street leading to Campbell Square on your left. A diversion into this space offers an interesting insight into recent warehouse regeneration and the creation of new open space and sculpture. Return to where the trail started.

Link to Trail 3: From the Chinese Arch go up Upper Duke Street to the Cathedral Gate.

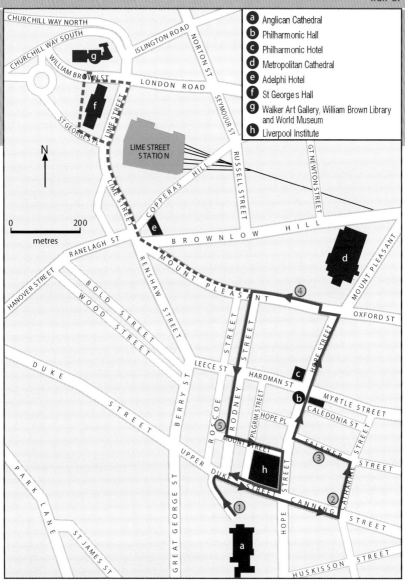

a Anglican Cathedral
b Philharmonic Hall
c Philharmonic Hotel
d Metropolitan Cathedral
e Adelphi Hotel
f St George's Hall
g Walker Art Gallery, William Brown Library and World Museum
h Liverpool Institute

Trail 3: Cinematic streetscapes

Distance: 2.2km
(3.3km incl extension)

Walking time: 1 hour 15
(2 hours 15 incl extension)

Disabled access: yes

It may come as a surprise to learn that Liverpool has the greatest number of listed buildings outside London, possesses one of the country's finest collections of eighteenth-century buildings, and has the highest proportion of urban greenspace in the UK. Yet, the popular image of Liverpool is as a city associated with ships, music and

Between the two Cathedrals.

© Jefferson's Air Photography

football, rather than the high quality of much of its built environment. In recent years several locations in the city have been favoured by film-makers, and many TV and film viewers will have seen Liverpool but may not be aware of it. Liverpool is in fact the most filmed city outside London, particularly favoured by producers of historical dramas.

This trail explores some of the locations which have featured in films and on television. It also visits some of the city's most visually impressive, imposing buildings in the vicinity of the two cathedrals and Mount Pleasant.

The trail starts at the Anglican Cathedral Church of Christ at the southern end of Hope Street. For most of its history Liverpool did not have a cathedral or its own diocese. However, during the nineteenth century the church authorities decided that the city should have both a diocese and an Anglican (Church of England) cathedral to reflect the city's importance. The Gothic-style, sandstone

cathedral was designed by Sir Giles Gilbert Scott (who was only 21 years old at the time that the architectural competition for the design of the cathedral was held in 1901). Building started in 1904 but was not finished until 1972. It is the largest Anglican cathedral in the world, the fifth largest cathedral building in the world, has the highest cathedral tower, the tallest cathedral arches and the largest church organ in the world.

Looking from the tower towards the River Mersey to the west it is possible to see the Wirral peninsula and, on a clear day, the Clwydian mountains in Wales.

Immediately adjacent to the cathedral grounds on the western side are some red-brick contemporary buildings which were built during the earliest attempts at inner city regeneration in the 1980s and largely initiated in 'Project Rosemary' by the Church Commissioners (Church of England).

© Mersey Partnership

Philarmonic Hall.

© Janet Speake/Vivien Fox

1. Leave the main entrance to the cathedral and walk down to Upper Duke Street, turning right up the hill into Canning Street, crossing Hope Street.

2. Turn left into Catharine Street. Continue (northwards) to Falkner Street and turn left. The streets in this area contain excellent examples of late eighteenth/early nineteenth century Georgian, largely residential, architecture (particularly Falkner Street). These houses were mainly built for merchants and wealthy residents of the city at the height of the port's prosperity. Most of the houses here are still lived in (although some of the larger properties are subdivided into apartments).

   Much of the streetscape has been extensively renovated to restore and enhance its historic character – note the old street lamps and stone paving flags. These features are not genuinely old but are part of the 'heritagisation' process associated with the city's wish to conserve its architectural legacy, which also makes it a valuable location for film-making. The Liverpool Film Office has been successful in attracting many film makers to the city. For example, in recent years this area has been used for film locations in the Forsyte Saga and Sherlock Holmes. Interestingly, this part of the city has often been used to represent Georgian London, not Liverpool.

3. Continue left along Falkner Street to the junction with Hope Street, turn right into Hope Street and continue northwards to a large grey-brick building on the right. This is the Modernist-style Philharmonic Hall (1933), the venue for concerts and home of the Royal Liverpool Philharmonic Orchestra. Diagonally opposite across Hope Street is the Philharmonic Hotel. This art nouveau style public house was built in 1900 and is one of the most ornate and flamboyant pubs in the country.

   Continue northwards along Hope Street past the Everyman Theatre (rebuilt in the 1960s and now a leading repertory theatre company) to the Metropolitan Cathedral.

   Liverpool's Metropolitan Cathedral of Christ the King is the city's Catholic cathedral within the Archdiocese of Liverpool, for which the site was bought by the Catholic Church in the 1930s. The original design by Sir Edwin Lutyens was for an imposing

Metropolitan Cathedral.

Romanesque-style cathedral with a great dome and barrel-vaulted naves and aisles. Building started in 1939 and the extensive crypt was soon completed. However, building was interrupted during the Second World War and afterwards the designs were changed. A smaller, less expensive building, designed by Sir Frederick Gibberd, was constructed and consecrated in 1967. It is built in the round and has a high central tower which is funnel-like in shape to allow light to flow into the building from above.

4. On leaving the cathedral from the southern steps, walk down the hill (Mount Pleasant) to the junction and turn left into Rodney Street.

    For those interested in discovering more of Liverpool's greatest buildings it is possible to extend the trail at this point to St George's Plateau. Follow Mount Pleasant down the hill, turn right past the Adelphi Hotel (1912), which was built to provide accommodation for passengers using the great liners, and Liverpool Lime Street Station (the city's main railway station). Opposite the station is the St George's Hall (opened 1854), a Grade 1 listed building which contains magnificent mosaic flooring. To the north of the St

George's Hall is the Walker Art Gallery (1877), famous for its collection of nineteenth-century Pre-Raphaelite paintings, and the William Brown Library and World Museum (1860). Return via Mount Pleasant to rejoin the main trail at Rodney Street.

The classically-proportioned Georgian buildings in Rodney Street date from the late eighteenth/early nineteenth centuries when this was a prestigious and expensive residential area at the then edge of the city. British Prime Minister William Gladstone and Dr W. Duncan, who became Liverpool's first public health officer in 1847 (Liverpool was the first city in the world to have its own public health officer), were both born in houses in Rodney Street. Today, most of the houses, which are among the most expensive in the city, are occupied by businesses, particularly doctors' and dentists' practices (it is the Liverpool equivalent of London's Harley Street). There are also some other imposing buildings in the street, such as the derelict shell of St Andrew's Church.

5. Continue along Rodney Street then turn left into Mount Street. On the right is the Liverpool Institute (1837). It was built as an institute

Trail 4.

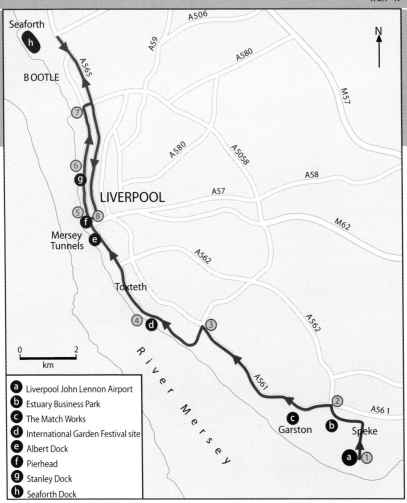

a Liverpool John Lennon Airport
b Estuary Business Park
c The Match Works
d International Garden Festival site
e Albert Dock
f Pierhead
g Stanley Dock
h Seaforth Dock

for engineers and later became a school for boys. Amongst its former students in the 1950s were Paul McCartney and George Harrison of the Beatles. The school closed in the 1980s and was re-opened in 1996 as the Liverpool Institute of Performing Arts. Sir Paul McCartney gave a large donation to help the project.

Turn right into Hope Street and return to the start of the trail at the Anglican Cathedral.

Trail 4: Regenerating Liverpool's Waterfront

Distance: 27km (31km with extension to Seaforth Dock)
Travel time: Half day by car
Disabled access: yes

The theme of this trail is the revitalisation of Liverpool's waterfront from John Lennon International Airport south of the city to the northern docks in Bootle. During the 1980s Liverpool's once flourishing docks experienced rapid economic decline and population loss due to the impacts of industrial and

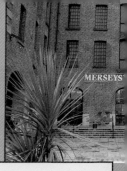

Trail 4 – Detail (a).

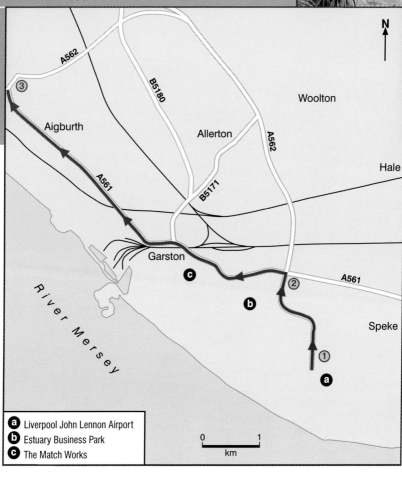

- **ⓐ** Liverpool John Lennon Airport
- **ⓑ** Estuary Business Park
- **ⓒ** The Match Works

economic restructuring, with the result that much of the land became vacant and derelict. Liverpool is not unique in how it has tackled its problem waterfront areas, but it was one of the first cities in the UK to try to revitalise its former docks using ideas developed in Boston and Baltimore in the USA.

Among the first waterfront projects in Liverpool were the revitalisation of the Albert Dock, and the International Garden Festival in 1984. Much of this regeneration was undertaken by the Merseyside Development Corporation (MDC) (1981-1997) and by various partnerships.

Regeneration of the waterfront has occurred in a series of phases. In the 1980s the emphasis was mainly on environmental improvements, heritage (e.g. museums such as the Maritime Museum at the Albert Dock), and residential developments. By the early twenty-first century the focus had shifted to regeneration driven by culturally-led initiatives (both popular and high culture), retailing and property development.

The impacts of regeneration on Liverpool's cityscape have been substantial and much of the waterfront has been transformed, particularly in the area south of Pier Head.

Liverpool's waterfront looking towards Speke.

1. The trail begins at Liverpool John Lennon International Airport. The airport is one of the most rapidly expanding airports in Europe and in 2002 became the fastest growing airport in the UK. In 2003, 3.18 million people travelled through the airport. Its rapid development has been largely due to the traffic generated by low-cost airlines like Easyjet and Ryanair which operate from here.

   Adjacent to the airport is Speke, a large housing estate constructed by the City Council in the 1930s. Like neighbouring Garston, Speke has experienced the effects of economic decline and high unemployment levels. There are major regeneration initiatives in the area that were set up by the Speke-Garston Partnership Regeneration Programme (now the Speke-Garston Development Company) in 1995. They were funded largely by the Single Regeneration Budget (SRB) and European Union Objective 1 finance.

2. On leaving the airport follow Speke Hall Avenue to the next major junction and turn left into Speke Road (A561) following signs for the city centre. The trail then continues on the A561 for the next 5.6km and key points of interest are as follows:

The Estuary Business Park
Constructed on the site of the former Liverpool Airport this attracts many commercial businesses to the area. The former airport terminal has been converted into an up-market hotel and one of the old aircraft hangars is now a leisure and sports club.

The revitalisation of retail premises in the area
This has focused on the Mersey Retail Park, which contains many well-known high street stores and so presents a challenge to the city centre as an alternative shopping destination. Opposite the entrance to the Mersey Retail Park is the Matchworks (the former Bryant & May match factory closed 1994) and its associated estate housing.

Trail 4 – Detail (b).

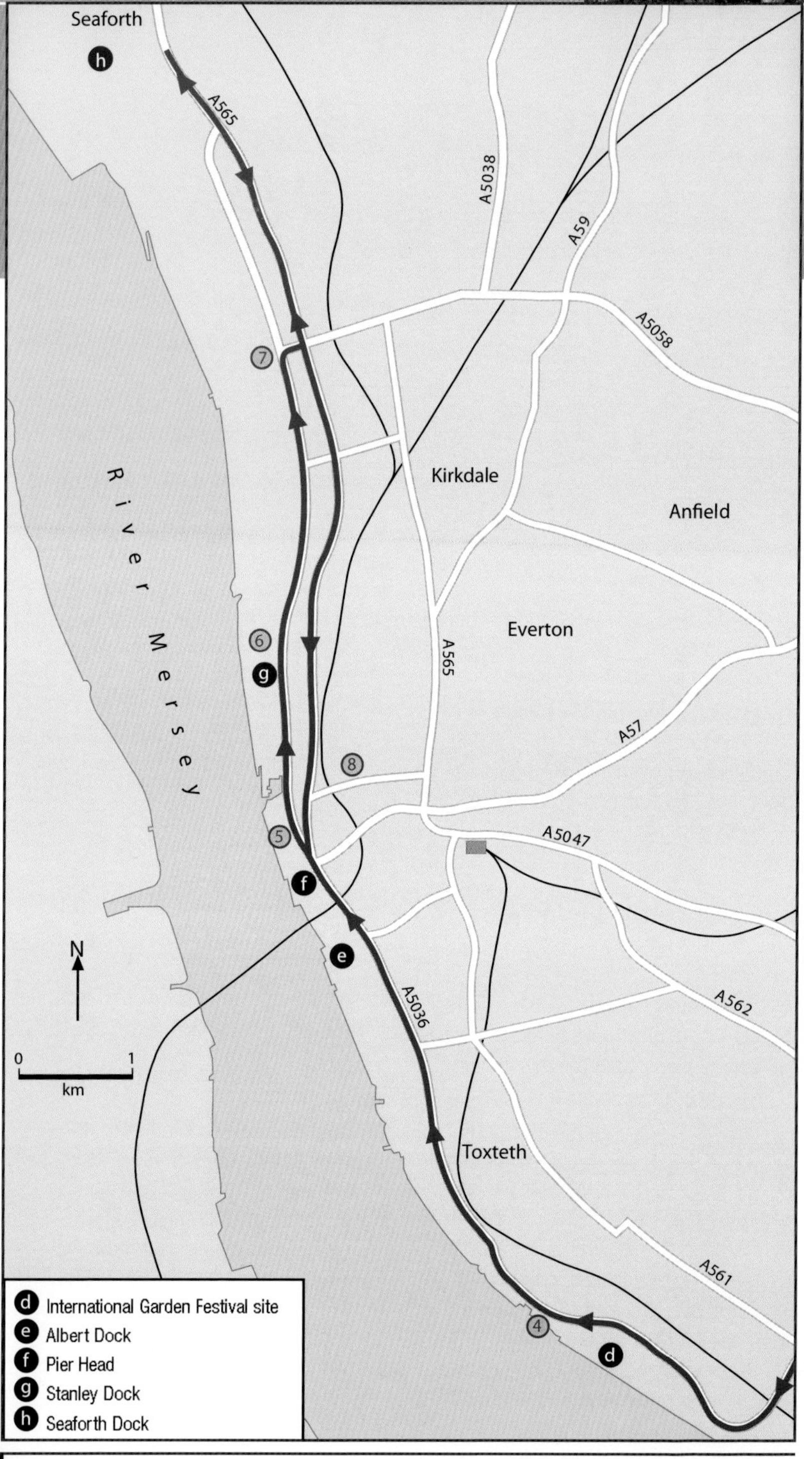

Seaforth

h

A565

A5038

A59

A5058

⑦

Kirkdale

Anfield

River Mersey

⑥

g

Everton

A565

⑧

A57

A5047

⑤

f

N

e

A5036

0 ___ 1
km

A562

Toxteth

A561

④

d

d	International Garden Festival site
e	Albert Dock
f	Pier Head
g	Stanley Dock
h	Seaforth Dock

Albert Dock.

Garston Docks

Established in 1846, these docks are still operational. From here the trail moves into the residential area of Grassendale with Grassendale Park, an affluent nineteenth-century estate, on the left. The broad, green, central reservation of the road marks the path of one of Liverpool's former tram routes.

3. Shortly after entering Aigburth turn left at a major crossroads into Jericho Lane (signed Liverpool Docks and Central Attractions). At Otterspool Promenade turn right into Riverside Drive.

   The first major improvements to this part of Liverpool's waterfront were made for the International Garden Festival in 1984, the effects of which can still be seen in the landscaping of the area. As part of the festival this section of the waterfront was opened up and made accessible through the creation of a promenade 'Riverside Walk' which links Otterspool to the city centre. The aim of the festival was to restore a derelict, contaminated part of the shore, create gardens and organise a summer-long festival. The restoration and the festival were successful but subsequent uses of the site have been short-lived and in 2004 it became vacant. The large, detached housing which borders the site was constructed after the festival.

4. Immediately to the north of the festival site and the Britannia pub is a riverside lay-by on the left and a car park on the right. On the promenade at this point is a series of sculptures in the shape of ship's funnels, each painted to reflect some of Liverpool's most prestigious shipping lines. Here too are views south across the River Mersey to the Wirral. The oil terminals at Eastham to the left and the tall buildings of the former Cammell Laird shipbuilding company to the right are readily identifiable.

   Between here and the city centre is a series of former quays and docks which have been revitalised in different ways. Columbus Quay is a residential complex centred on

Liver Building.

© Mersey Partnership

waterfront apartments. Herculaneum Dock is an infilled dock occupied by various commercial enterprises, e.g. leisure facilities. Coburg Quay's extensive residential area (mostly purpose-built apartments) is located adjacent to a number of water-based amenities such as the marina and the award-winning watersports centre at the Coburg and Brunswick Docks. Brunswick Dock has been transformed into a commercial area with converted warehouses and new buildings.

The 'Dock Road' which links these developments has become known locally as 'Motor Mile' because of the large number of car dealerships which have moved into the area.

The contrasts between the extensive regeneration activities that have taken place along the waterfront here and the more traditional inner city areas immediately inland (e.g. Dingle) are still quite marked.

The major development at the Queen's Dock has been the construction of offices that are occupied by a number of organisations such as the national VAT (tax) Office and the Charities Commission. Since the 1980s the King's Dock has been used as a car park and as a temporary location for the 'Summer Proms' (when concerts are held in a large marquee). Proposals for the site include various combinations of concert venues, commercial premises and housing.

5. Continue past the Albert Dock, Pier Head and the Liver Building (left) to a forked junction. Take the left fork A5036 (signposted Docks). The regenerated Princes Dock has a range of uses including hotels which are able to take advantage of the dock's city centre location. The Waterloo Docks warehouse (1869) has been converted into apartments and during the 1990s were the most northerly of the docks to be revitalised in this way.

North of the Waterloo Docks the extensive docklands are either vacant, awaiting revitalisation, e.g. Stanley Dock, or are still fully operational as docks, e.g. Canada

Tobacco Warehouse, Stanley Dock.

Dock and Seaforth Terminal. A number of the dry docks are used for ship repair and maintenance. Glimpses of Liverpool's scrap metal trade can also be seen in the large and extensive mounds of metal that line parts of the waterfront.

6. Stanley Dock is Liverpool's only inland dock and accounts for the lifting road bridge at this point. From here until Canada Dock it is often possible to pull in alongside the road. Access to the river is via the Collingwood Dock and Salisbury Dock. Stanley Dock's warehouses on the south side of the dock date from 1848 and were designed by Jesse Hartley (who was also architect for the Albert Dock). At the eastern end of the dock is the entrance to the Leeds-Liverpool Canal. The Stanley Dock Tobacco Warehouse (1900) on the dock's south side is 11 storeys high. One of the distinctive features of the structure is the comparatively small vertical distance between the windows, which reflects the low ceiling heights, a fire-prevention feature of the building and one which has presented problems in relation to its conversion or re-use.

The dock wall which separates the docks and quays from the road is a distinctive feature of the northern docks at this point. From here to Sandon Dock it is c. 6m high and constructed of granite.

The large scale of the contemporary dock operations can be clearly seen at Canada Dock which mostly handles containers. From here there are views ahead to Seaforth Dock. Seaforth Terminal was constructed in 1971 and is now, like most of the active docks in Liverpool and Wirral, operated by the Mersey Docks and Harbour Company. It is a containerised facility and can accommodate ships of up to 75,000 tons. It handles a wide range of goods including grain and timber, and trades with destinations around the world, including North America, northern Europe and the Mediterranean.

7. Just past Canada Dock turn right into Millers Bridge Road and continue to the junction with the A5080. At this point:

Freeport at Seaforth.

© Janet Speake/Vivien Fox

PORT OF LIVERPOOL & *FREEPORT*

either turn right at traffic lights into Derby Road to return to Liverpool city centre,

or turn left at traffic lights to extend the trail (by c. 3km) to the entrance of the Seaforth Dock. Follow signs to Freeport and at the roundabout in front of Freeport follow signs for A565 Liverpool.

The A565 from the northern docks to Liverpool has been improved – notice the new street furniture and landscaping – in order to attract new businesses to the area. Part of it has been renamed 'Atlantic Boulevard'.

8. At the junction with the inner ring road turn right into King Edward Street (A5027) and follow signs for Pier Head on the A5036. Take the first entrance (right turn) for the Albert Dock near the Pumphouse. If you wish to now follow Trail 1, parking is available on the south side of the dock buildings.

The Grade I listed Albert Dock (built 1841-45) was renovated in the 1980s after several years of decline and decay and is one of the UK's earliest examples of waterfront regeneration. The restoration programme focused on the dock buildings and maritime heritage, and Tate Liverpool, The Beatles Story, shops and bars were among the early attractions for visitors. Its regeneration also included the conversion of the warehouse buildings into apartments. In the 1990s the Albert Dock experienced an economic downturn and many of the shops closed or relocated. However, at the end of the decade the dock was 're-regenerated', the Tate Liverpool was refurbished, new bars, clubs and exclusive shops were opened and the Dock has since experienced an economic revival.

Bibliography and further information

© Mersey Partnership

Bibliography

Bailey, F.A. and Millington, R. (1957) *The Story of Liverpool*. Liverpool: The Corporation of Liverpool.

Chandler, G. (1957) *Liverpool*. London: Batsford.

Chandler, G. (1960) *Liverpool Shipping: A short history*. London: Phoenix House.

Cresswell, R.K. and Lawton, R. (1964) *Merseyside*. Sheffield: Geographical Association.

Fox, V. (1996) 'Planning issues on Merseyside: the challenge for the 1990s' in Erdeli, G. and Chambers, W.J. (1996) *Proceedings of the First Romanian-British Geographic Seminar*, University of Bucharest, pp. 83-95.

Frayman, H. (1991) *Breadline Britain – 1990s: The findings of the television series*. London: Domino Films and London Weekend Television.

Gould, T.S. and Hodgkiss, A.G. (eds) (1982) *The Resources of Merseyside*. Liverpool: The University of Liverpool.

Hyde, F.E. (1971) *Liverpool and the Mersey: An economic history of a port 1700-1970*. Newton Abbott: David and Charles.

Hughes, Q. (1999) *Liverpool City of Architecture*. Liverpool: Blue Coat Press.

Jones, R. (1992) *The American Connection* (second edition). Wirral: Ron Jones.

Lawton, R. and Cunningham, C.M. (1970) *Merseyside: Social and economic studies*. Harlow: Longman.

Liverpool City Council (1993) *Key Statistics: Liverpool Wards 1971/81/91*. Liverpool: Liverpool City Council.

Liverpool City Council (2005) *Census 2001: Key statistics for Liverpool*. Liverpool: The City of Liverpool Regeneration Policy Division.

Liverpool City Council and Liverpool Vision (2004) *Regeneration and Development in Liverpool City Centre 1995-2004*. Liverpool: Liverpool City Council and Liverpool Vision.

Liverpool City Planning Department (1990) *Liverpool Heritage Walks*. Liverpool: Liverpool City Planning Department and Bluecoat Press.

Liverpool Heritage Bureau (1978) *Buildings of Liverpool*. Liverpool: Liverpool City Planning Department.

Morris, C. (ed) (1984) *The Illustrated Journeys of Celia Fiennes, c.1682-1712*. London: Macdonald/Webb and Bower, pp. 160-61.

Munck, R. (ed) (2003) *Reinventing the City? Liverpool in Comparative Perspective*. Liverpool: Liverpool University Press.

Sharples, J. (2004) *Liverpool (Pevsner Architectural City Guides)*. Yale, CT: Yale University Press.

The Mersey Partnership (2003) *Mersey Economic Review Summary*. Merseyside: The Mersey Partnership.

Woodhouse, G. in association with Cities500 (2004) *Liverpool World Heritage City*. Liverpool: Cities500.

Further Information

Tourist Information Centres

Liverpool Tourist Information Centre, Queens Square, Liverpool L1 1RG
Tel: 0151 709 5111

Liverpool Tourist Information Centre, Atlantic Pavilion, Albert Dock, Liverpool L3 4AE
Tel: 0151 709 5111

Liverpool Tourist Information Centre, Liverpool John Lennon Airport, Speke Hall Avenue, Liverpool L24 1YD
Tel: 0151 709 5111

Maps

OS Landranger *108 Liverpool* (1:50,000)

OS Explorer *275 Liverpool, St Helens, Widnes and Runcorn* (1:25,000)

Geographer's A-Z Map Company *A-Z Street Atlas Liverpool* (1:15,840)

Local Studies Library

Liverpool City Library, Central Library,
William Brown Street, Liverpool L3 8EW
Tel: 0151 233 5858

Websites

BBC Merseyside
http://www.bbc.co.uk/liverpool

B&W Picture Place
http://www.bwpics.co.uk

European Union and Merseyside
http://www.euandmerseyside.org

Liverpool City Council
http://www.liverpool.gov.uk

Liverpool John Lennon Airport
http://www.liverpooljohnlennonairport.com

Liverpool Vision (Regeneration Agency)
http://www.liverpoolvision.com

Mersey Docks and Harbour Company
http://www.merseydocks.co.uk

Mersey Gateway
http://www.merseyside-gateway.org

Mersey Partnership
http://www.merseyside.org.uk

National Museums and Galleries on
Merseyside
http://www.nmgm.org.uk

National Statistics Online
http://www.statistics.gov.uk

North West Development Agency
http://www.nwda.co.uk

Pennine Waterways
http://www.penninewaterways.co.uk

Urban Splash
http://www.urbansplash.co.uk

Wells Mackereth Architects
http://www.wellsmackereth.com

Photo credits

Black & White Picture Place

Chris Tubbs

Everton Football Club

Janet Speake and Vivien Fox

Jefferson's Air Photography

John Mills Photography

Liverpool City Council

Liverpool Daily Post & Echo Syndication Dept

Liverpool Football Club

Liverpool John Lennon Airport

Mersey Partnership

National Archive

Pennine Waterways

Richard Cooper, Photoflex